WALKS
SURREY

WALKS IN THE SURREY HILLS

Janet Spayne and
Audrey Krynski

FREDERICK WARNE

FREDERICK WARNE

Published by the Penguin Group
27 Wrights Lane, London W8 5TZ England
Viking Penguin Inc., 40 West 23rd Street, New York, New York 10010, USA
Penguin Books Australia Ltd, Ringwood, Victoria, Australia
Penguin Books Canada Ltd, 2801 John Street, Markham, Ontario, Canada L3R 1B4
Penguin Books (NZ) Ltd, 182–190 Wairau Road, Auckland 10, New Zealand

Penguin Books Ltd, Registered Offices: Harmondsworth, Middlesex, England

First published 1974
2nd edition 1975
3rd edition 1976
4th edition 1979
5th edition 1983
6th edition 1988

Publisher's Note

At the time of publication all the walks in this book were made along paths designated as official footpaths, but it should be borne in mind that diversion orders may be made from time to time, and neither the Authors nor the Publisher can accept responsibility for those who stray from the Rights of Way.

ISBN 0 7232 3531 7

Printed and bound in Great Britain by
Cox & Wyman Ltd, Reading

CONTENTS

Introduction

Walk 1 The Silent Pool, St Martha's, Chilworth—2 walks 9

Walk 2 Chilworth, Shamley Green, Wonersh—1 walk 13

Walk 3 Gomshall, Shere Heath, Albury Park, Blackheath, Brook—2 walks 17

Walk 4 Windmill Hill, Reynards Hill, Winterfold Heath, Helmet Copse, Dicks Hill—1 walk 23

Walk 5 Peaslake, Holmbury Hill and Pitch Hill—1 walk 27

Walk 6 Westcott, Broomy Down, Townhurst Wood, The Rookery—1 walk 31

Walk 7 Friday Street, Abinger Bottom, High Ashes, Holmbury St Mary, Pasture Wood—1 walk 35

Walk 8 Horsley, Sheepleas—1 walk 39

Walk 9 Mountain Wood and Netley Heath—1 walk 43

Walk 10 Ranmore, Six Acre Copse, High Barn, Yewtree Farm, Pigdon—1 walk 47

Walk 11 From Boxhill Station through Ranmore and Polesden Lacey Woods—1 walk 51

Walk 12 Dorking, Deepdene, Betchworth Golf Course, Glory Wood—1 walk 55

Walk 13 Leith Hill, Redlands, Anstiebury Farm, Kitlands—1 walk 59

Walk 14   Headley Heath, Mickleham Downs—1 walk   63

Walk 15   Headley and Headley Heath—1 walk   67

Walk 16   Boxhill, Brockham Hills, Duke's Plantation,
               Juniper Top, The Whites—2 walks   71

Walk 17   Reigate Hill, Colley Hill—2 walks   77

Walk 18   Chipstead Valley and Long Plantation—1 walk   81

Walk 19   Coulsdon, Happy Valley and Chaldon—1 walk   85

Walk 20   Chelsham, Woldingham—1 walk   89

INTRODUCTION

We have compiled this collection of walks from an intimate knowledge of the North Downs area acquired over the last fifteen years or so through exploring the countryside together, having met as fellow members of the Ramblers Association. Our rambling activities have opened up a new world for us, giving us an interest in map-reading, in the changing seasons, each of which has its own particular advantages, in animal and insect life and, above all, in plant life. Identification of an unusual flower or tree leads us to reference books and not merely increases our knowledge but our interest in the beautiful countryside of Surrey.

Surrey has some of the widest variety of country to be found in England—farmland, heathland, woods, water and downland and a large number of areas of outstanding natural beauty. The walks in this book explore only a small part of Surrey and for the most part we have avoided the well-trodden ways to share some of the smaller more obscure paths which we have discovered in our wanderings. Sheets 186 and 187 of the new O.S. 1:50.000 maps will cover all the walks but a $2\frac{1}{2}''$ map gives a lot more detail and although not essential will greatly add to your enjoyment in following the routes. The sketch maps included in the text are not to any scale but merely give a rough indication of the direction of the walks.

To any who feel themselves afflicted with middle-age boredom when family ties are no longer so demanding, we heartily recommend that they take up rambling and, as we do, set aside a regular day each week to explore the countryside, ideally with one or two friends. For those of all ages we recommend this stimulating occupation as an antidote to the stresses and strains of modern urban life.

AUDREY KRYNSKI

JANET SPAYNE

THE SILENT POOL

St Martha's, Chilworth
6 miles (or two walks of 3 miles each)

This ramble in the Tillingbourne Valley takes us through woodland, downland and farmland. We see the remains of the gunpowder industry for which Chilworth was once famous and pass the mill ponds with their wild life. Very little mud will be encountered.

How to get there: By 773 Green Line or 417 Sunday Ramblers bus from Dorking to the junction of A25 and A248. Or by train to Chilworth where the walk can be joined. By car to the car park at The Silent Pool.

If Chilworth is the starting point
Leaving Chilworth Station we turn left along the main road for approximately 100 yards when we take a footpath on the right next to a school. We cross a bridge over the river, taking the right fork to a crossing track where we turn right, keeping straight ahead to a high bank of earth. Now we continue the walk from (X).

If only a 3 mile walk from Chilworth is desired
Follow the walk to (B) and then turn to (A)—the signposted bridleway on the right referred to at (A) is of course the same left path at (B).

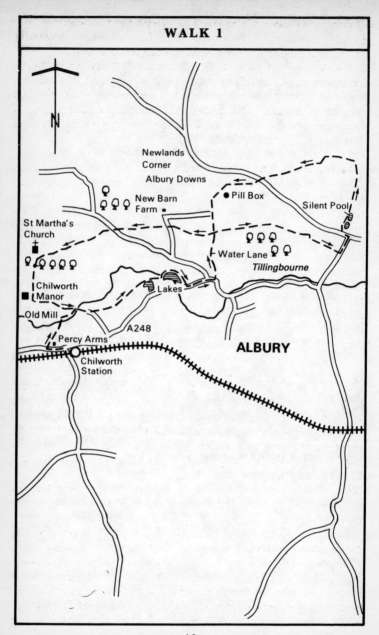

If only a 3 mile walk from The Silent Pool is desired

Follow the walk to (A) and then turn to (C)—the left-hand turning at (A) is of course the same right-hand turning at (C).

If returning to Chilworth Station or needing Chilworth for refreshment at (X) instead of turning left by the bank of earth, we continue forward and where the woods open out we take the first turning on the left to a bridge over the river continuing on a footpath up to the road by a school. Here we turn left for *The Percy Arms* and Chilworth Station.

Starting from The Silent Pool

After visiting The Silent Pool, which is fed by strong underground springs and very deep, we return to the entrance and turn right on the track with the Pool on our right, going uphill for nearly half a mile to a wide crossing track at the top of the hill where we turn left. Later when this forks we take the left, slightly downhill track, and keep left again at the next fork. At this point views of Hascombe Hill can be seen on the skyline. We come out to a road which we cross slightly right to a small footpath, turning right at first keeping parallel with the road. At a junction of paths, with a pillbox on the left, we turn left down a stony track, bearing left just past an old quarry, and continue down the lane passing a turning on the right which goes to New Barn Farm.

(A) A few yards past a turning on the left we take the signposted bridleway on the right, later going through a gate and along the edge of a field. At the end of the field we turn right along the hedge to a gate on the left into a lane. We take the track opposite with a blue waymark and continue along this pilgrims' trackway between wooden fences out to a road. We cross the road to a path slightly to the left and go left with it, turning right through a barrier and forking right uphill, ignoring all branching paths until St Martha's Church is reached.

The original church dated from the late 12th century but fell into disrepair and was rebuilt on its original foundations in the mid-19th century.

Leaving the church by the south wicket gate between conifers, opposite the entrance to the church, we take a steep downhill path after ignoring a crossing track. At the end of this footpath we turn right to look at Chilworth Manor. There is a local legend that a tunnel once ran between the Manor and St Martha's Church. Retracing our steps we continue along the signposted bridleway which eventually becomes a lane. Just after passing a farm entrance

11

on the left we turn right into woods, shortly turning left by a high bank of earth.

(X) We keep on this path with the Tillingbourne on our right, and on our left we pass the ruins of a gunpowder mill with trees growing up from ground floor to a height well above roof level. From the mid 17th century until the end of the First World War Chilworth was an important centre for the gunpowder industry. These woods are full of old mill stones and remains of other mills, and in the 1914–18 war a regiment of soldiers kept guard day and night on the various buildings.

Passing the mill buildings on our left we return to the lane where we turn right over the bridge and immediately left over a stile. We cross a meadow diagonally to another stile, keeping parallel with a wet ditch on our right, then over another stile and plank bridge into a field, and straight ahead with a wire fence on the right. Another stile takes us into a private garden which has the public footpath running close to the fence on the right. We come out into a lane where we turn left and round the edge of the lake passing a mill. The path bears left at the end of the first lake round to another lake. We turn right at the cottage on a rising footpath with the lake on our right, then go through a barrier, keeping forward on the footpath through cottage gardens and out into the main road.

We turn left in the road and take the second turning on the left into Water Lane. We go along here for about half a mile to a signpost on the left (B) and just beyond is a turning to the right (C) which we take, passing a few houses. This becomes a grassy track and passes an isolated cottage on the right. We continue forward over a stile and soon take a signposted footpath ahead. At the end of this path we cross a sandy track to a small path opposite with a wooden hut on the right. We bear right behind the hut with a fence on the left and soon climb over a stile on the left. Following the fence across a field we come to a road where we turn left and are soon at the main road which we cross to the left to the house at the entrance to The Silent Pool.

Refreshments: There is an inn at Chilworth.

CHILWORTH

Chilworth, Shamley Green, Wonersh
$7\frac{3}{4}$ miles

This is a ramble in woodland and over heather- and gorse-covered
heathland, visiting two of Surrey's pretty villages, Shamley Green
and Wonersh, with their 16th and 17th century houses. The walk
is recommended for any time of the year and while there are
bluebells in spring and heather in high summer, it is perhaps at its
best on a crisp winter day with hoar frost on the ground.

How to get there: By train or No. 25 bus from Guildford to Chilworth
Station. By car on the A248 (off the A25) to Chilworth Station,
turning left up Sampleoak Lane to a crossroads, turning left again
to a large car park.
    From the car park we return to the crossroads and keep ahead
to the end of houses and at the *Blackheath* sign on the right we turn
left.

From the station we turn left up Sampleoak Lane for about half a
mile. There is a parallel footpath on the left of the road. We pass a
Franciscan Friary on the right and continue to the *Blackheath* sign
where we turn right into a wide bridleway and soon turn left on a
path across a heather-covered common. At a T junction we turn
right into a sandy track soon coming to a crossing track where we
turn left and then straight ahead, ignoring a right fork, till the
path bears left, passes some houses and leads us out to a road.

13

WALK 2

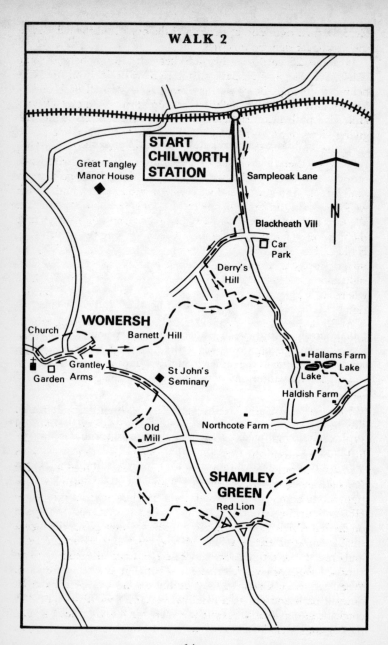

START
CHILWORTH
STATION

Great Tangley
Manor House

Sampleoak Lane

N

Blackheath Vill

Car
Park

Derry's
Hill

WONERSH

Barnett Hill

Church

Grantley
Arms

Garden

St John's
Seminary

Hallams Farm
Lake

Lake

Haldish Farm

Old
Mill

Northcote Farm

SHAMLEY
GREEN

Red Lion

Here we turn right and at the end of the houses on the left and at the *Blackheath* sign we turn left.

In about 25 yards, as this lane bears left to go behind some houses, we take a small path on the right with fields on the right behind the hedge. Soon we take the first very small path on the left, initially lined with holly bushes, uphill to the top of Derry's Hill. The path bears right taking us along the ridge of the hill, giving views of St Martha's Church on the hill on the left.

At the wide T junction we turn right and keep ahead, forking right when there is a choice to a crossing track and a wire fence round a plantation which we keep on our right as we go along a sandy track. At a gate ahead we turn left into a sunken path which we follow with the fence on our right until we reach a minor road. We turn right along the road and just past farm buildings we take the signposted footpath to Darbyns Brook, passing the picturesque Hallams Farm on the left. Continuing along the gravel drive we turn right past a lake and left past a beautiful house where we turn right along a hedged track. This brings us out to a tarmac lane where we turn right passing the attractive Haldish Farm on our right.

At Blackmoor Lodge we take a footpath on the left going gradually uphill to a crossing bridleway on Reelhall Hill. Here we turn right and immediately left thus continuing direction downhill. After two stiles in quick succession we cross a field diagonally to two more stiles in the corner, then go down a narrow hedged path to the road.

Here we turn right for Shamley Green, a village built round two triangular village greens, most of the houses being 16th and 17th century. On reaching the first green we turn right with the little pond on our left then turn right along the next green with *The Red Lion* on our right. We bear left across the green from *The Red Lion* and go down Sweetwater Lane. In a few yards we turn right along an enclosed footpath soon bearing right, into Nursery Hill, and turning left uphill. At No. 42 there is an enclosed footpath on the left which soon leaves the houses and after going through a small plantation enters a field. We ignore the stiles on the right and cross the field to the far corner and another stile leading to an enclosed footpath which crosses a drive and continues forward. When we reach Cherry Tree Cottage on the left we turn right down a path and out to a road, where again we turn right. We continue along this pleasant little road for less than half a mile passing some delightful houses, and as the road turns sharply right we go through a kissing gate to a footpath on the left. We keep straight ahead, crossing a mill stream and turning right with the drive past the 15th century Mill House.

We come out to the main road and turn left past St John's Seminary, taking the higher level path parallel with the road. Just past some steps on the right giving access to a house we turn right up the next steps into a field. We follow a well-defined path straight across the field to go through a kissing gate, turning left down to a timbered farmhouse. We then turn left down a minor road to the main road, turning right for the centre of Wonersh, passing the 15th century *Grantley Arms* on our left. From the centre of the village we take the road signposted to Bramley where there are many lovely black and white timbered houses. Through a brick archway on the left is a secluded garden given by Mrs F. H. Cook for the quiet use of the residents. Note the interesting friezes either side of the archway.

Just past the entrance to the church on our left we take a footpath on the right through a kissing gate by the side of a beautiful ancient timbered house. At the end of a brick wall we turn right through 'squeeze' posts down a track to a road, passing the Memorial Hall on our left. We cross the road diagonally left and with the Health Centre on our right follow the trees and a ditch on the right to another road where we turn right. In a few yards we take the signposted footpath on our left by the timbered farmhouse we passed earlier and continue along this fenced path gradually going uphill to the top of Barnett Hill. Soon after passing the house at the top of the hill we take an enclosed footpath on our right down to a stile leading into a fenced bridleway. We continue forward passing a small chapel and graveyard on our right and later some farm buildings on our left. At a junction of paths we turn left following the fence round on our left and continue along this path, returning to the lane we were in earlier, and out to the road. We then turn right and just past the Village Hall (for the car park keep straight on) take the signposted bridleway on our left, soon turning right on a track behind a house. Another track feeds in on the left and we are shortly at a crossing track where we turn right. After about 50 yards a narrow path turns off on our left, leading us to a track where we turn right into Sampleoak Lane and left for the station.

Refreshments are available at Shamley Green with a choice of inns. At Wonersh an inn and the little corner shop which sells ice cream.

16

GOMSHALL

Shere Heath, Albury Park. $4\frac{3}{4}$ miles
Shere Heath, Albury Heath, Blackheath, Brook. 7 miles

This is a heath, park and farmland walk taking us past many beautiful old houses. It is suitable for any time of the year and very little mud will be encountered in this mainly sandy area.

How to get there: By train or No. 417 or Green Line 773 bus to Gomshall Station where there is a car park.

For both walks:
Leaving Gomshall Station down the approach road we turn left in the main road under the railway bridge and immediately turn right along Wonham Way, a stony track. We cross a stream, pass a cottage on the left and as the track turns sharply left we turn right along a fenced path with a large house on the right and farm buildings on the left. At the end of the path we turn right under the railway bridge and then left along a small road to a junction. We go straight across to a signposted bridleway bearing left. Opposite a house called Old Barn on the left, we turn right with another house called Highlands on the right, keeping on the right-hand path between fences with views of Netley House up on the right. Soon coming into open fields with a hedge on the right we keep straight ahead noticing Shere Church down on our right. Our path comes out to a small residential road along which we continue

17

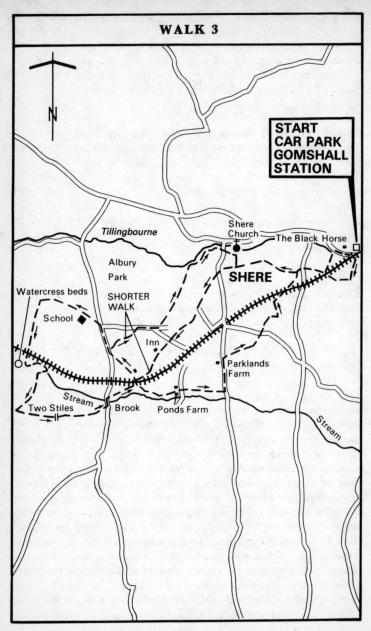

WALK 3

N

**START
CAR PARK
GOMSHALL
STATION**

Tillingbourne

Shere
Church

The Black Horse

SHERE

Albury

Park

**SHORTER
WALK**

Watercress beds

School

Inn

Parklands
Farm

Stream

Two Stiles

Stream

Brook

Ponds Farm

18

to another road at the *Shere* village sign where we cross to a signposted bridleway opposite, starting as a tarmac lane. This leads us through a small housing estate and into a fenced path which goes uphill into woods.

When the track forks we take the right-hand fork for a few yards only and then a small left-hand uphill path through pine trees on Shere Heath. At a fork either path may be used and we shortly come out to a small road which we cross to a track opposite taking the right fork until we soon reach an open space and junction of several paths. From here we take the first path on the right, later continuing over a clearing and a main crossing track and maintaining direction with a fringe of trees on the left. This path later drops down on the left to a sunken path and brings us out to the road at *The William IVth Inn* at Little London. We turn left down the road, taking a footpath on the right just before the railway bridge.

We go up this fenced path, through a barrier and on to Albury Heath, keeping straight ahead and passing a small red brick building on the right. We continue along the sandy track to a wider crossing track where we take the centre one of three paths ahead following it to a crossing track beyond a seat.

For the shorter version via Albury Park
We turn right on this crossing track, with houses down on the right, and quite soon at the next junction of paths take the left fork out to a road in which we turn right. We pass some houses on the right and as the road bears right we take a footpath on the left through a gate into Albury Park and down an avenue of fine chestnut trees, keeping on the main path over a stile and then to a gate by the lodge on the right. Keeping along the track with the river and ford on our left, and passing some delightful old houses on our right, we come out to the main street of the village of Shere. We cross the main street to a small road opposite leading to the church. At the end of the houses on the right and opposite the church we go through a gate and up a hedged path, at the end of which we turn left with a hedge on our left. Keeping on this path, along which we came earlier, we come to a lane in which we turn left and out to a road.

We cross this road to take the road signposted to Dorking, turning left at the railway bridge and out to the main road at

19

Gomshall Mill. Turning right in the main road we pass *The Black Horse* on the left and Gomshall Station is just beyond.

For the longer version over Blackheath and Brook

At the crossing track we turn left and as the path at once forks we keep right to a road and cross straight over, turning right at the edge of a playing field parallel with the road. We cross tracks leading to a pavilion and keeping the trees on our right we take a narrow and easily missed footpath in the right-hand corner into trees. This path takes us down to a wide sandy track which leads to a white cottage on the left but we go up a small path opposite to a clearing with school buildings on the left. Notice the chimneys which are characteristic of the old buildings in this area. Passing school buildings and a fence we turn left through a gate into a signposted bridleway. When this wide track divides we keep left, soon ignoring a downhill path on the right and continuing to a crossing path with stiles each side. We take the left-hand one and go through a plantation at the end of which is another stile into a field. Here we turn left towards two or three large trees, noticing on our right St Martha's Church on the top of the hill.

We go down the field and across the railway, continuing forward to a tree-lined sunken path which bears left to an attractive timbered farmhouse. After going through gates and between farm buildings we pass watercress beds on our right and come out to a lane where we turn right into a sandy uphill path. Near the top we take the first track on our left passing a large pine tree on the right. We keep left at the fork and at a crossing track go left between posts along a wide grassy track through a plantation. Crossing a stile we go downhill over a field maintaining direction to a footpath sign where we turn slightly left to a gate and across a green to a road at Brook.

We turn left in the road and over a stream then turn right into the lane to Shere and Peaslake, passing some delightful cottages, particularly Chennels built in 1636 with interesting wood carvings on the roof timbers. We keep along this little road to the railway bridge which we passed near earlier in the walk, and just before it take the signposted footpath on the right along a tarmac lane to Ponds Farm at the end. We cross the farm lane, go up some steps opposite and cross the centre of a field to trees and a road. Here we turn left and just past Parklands Farm on the left take a signposted footpath on the right between wire fences. At a wider track we turn left and out to a road where we turn right and almost immediately turn left along a gravel drive. Keeping straight ahead on an enclosed grassy track which bears right with a wall, at a gap we soon turn left across a field. Just before the hedge ahead the path forks and we take the right fork across to the corner of the field and join a bridleway crossing the railway. We continue down to a wider lane and keep straight ahead with Old Barn on the right, bearing right out to a road. Gomshall Station can be reached by crossing this road and taking the road signposted to Dorking. We turn left at the railway bridge and out to the main road at Gomshall Mill, turning right in the main road, passing *The Black Horse* on the left. Gomshall Station is just beyond.

Refreshments: Teas and morning coffee at Gomshall Mill. Inns at Little London, Shere and Gomshall.

WINDMILL HILL

**Reynards Hill, Winterfold Heath,
Helmet Copse, Dicks Hill. $4\frac{1}{2}$ miles**

This is a walk through heather, bilberries, pines and birches on
the less frequented hills west of Holmbury and Pitch Hill with
expansive views. Deer can frequently be seen and it is a good
walk for any time of the year.

How to get there: By car to Hurtwood Control car park 3 at the
southern end of Mill Bottom at the foot of Pitch Hill. Turn off the
A25 at Shere and the car park is four miles down on the left just
before reaching *The Windmill Inn.*

Leaving the car park we cross the road to an uphill track at the
side of Mill Cottage, avoiding a sunken path which bears right.
Our path resembles a gully at first but when we have reached the
top of Windmill Hill it leads us past a windmill, now used as a
residence, on our left. Ignoring tracks leading right, and passing
other buildings on our left we continue downhill and reach the
road at a fork. Between the forks is Hurtwood Control car park 4
and from this we take a footpath leading right. This fairly broad
track leads us through woods and out to a clearing at the top of
Reynards Hill where we can rest on a seat provided and admire
the view. Hascombe Hill can be seen on the right in the distance.
Continuing on our path, we ignore a right fork and eventually
wind our way out to the road where we take a path on the left

WALK 4

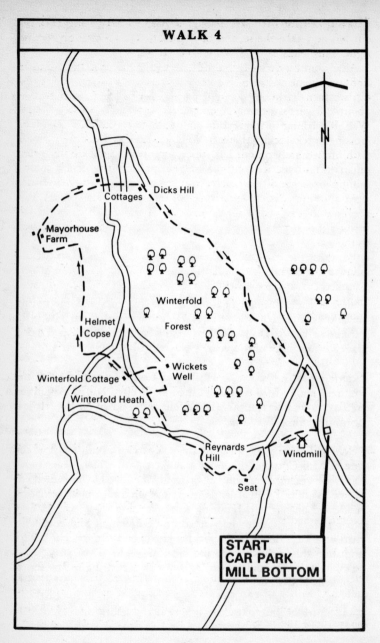

N

Dicks Hill

Cottages

Mayorhouse Farm

Winterfold Forest

Helmet Copse

Wickets Well

Winterfold Cottage

Winterfold Heath

Reynards Hill

Windmill

Seat

**START
CAR PARK
MILL BOTTOM**

parallel with the road. We rejoin the road with a sunken path on our left and take the second of two footpaths turning off on our right. This leads us over Winterfold Heath.

After about a quarter of a mile, at a junction of paths, we turn right on a wide path which goes down a dip. At the bottom of the dip we turn left along a small path between conifers, and after about 200 yards we emerge on a main crossing track at Wickets Well. Returning to where our small path emerged on to the main crossing track facing Wickets Well we take another very small path immediately on our left which soon bears right uphill. After our path flattens, we continue over a small crossing track, maintaining direction till we reach a wide crossing track where we turn right and immediately left, dropping to a slightly lower level. We are now at the hedge surrounding Winterfold Cottage and we turn right past the cottage continuing forward on the lane and out to the road.

We cross the road to a footpath opposite and keep forward to follow a line of trees on our right. After 100 yards or so, just before a sunken crossing track, we go over a signposted stile on our right and forward beside a wide, grassy "ride" and a conifer plantation known as Helmet Copse. We keep parallel with the sunken track down on our left for just over half a mile. At a crossing track we turn left into a hedged track leading to Mayorhouse Farm.

Just before the farmhouse itself we take a cart track on the right passing between farm buildings and noticing white doves around the barn on the left. At the end of the buildings we go over a stile, forward to another stile, and maintain direction to a third stile in the corner of the field. We drop down into an enclosed lane which we cross, going up the bank and over two stiles in quick succession. After continuing over several more stiles we reach the road at Shophouse Farm.

We turn left in the road and almost immediately right, along a signposted fenced footpath, then over a stile and across a wide drive to a barrier opposite, keeping straight ahead, passing a cottage named Pooh Corner. We go down some wooden steps and through a woodland path, over a ditch and bear left up to a sandy track with a cottage on the opposite side.

Here we cross a culvert and turn immediately right, with a telegraph pole on our left, into a path which we follow for over a mile, first with a stream and Dicks Hill on our left and later with the stream on our right. In dry weather the stream is practically non-existent and in wet weather it is inclined to overflow on to the footpath in places. The path is sometimes difficult to follow, but if we keep as near as possible to the stream or stream-bed we eventually come out on a crossing track. We cross to another wide track going uphill, a wide forestry track comes in on the right and we continue until we reach a gate and the road. We cross to a horse track among the trees and go forward bearing right with the track. Other tracks join ours from the left but we continue bearing right and going gradually uphill. We go over a major crossing track and continue forward till we reach the windmill where we turn left downhill, and out to the road by Mill Cottage opposite the car park.

PEASLAKE

Holmbury Hill and Pitch Hill
5 miles

This walk takes us through woods, gorse and heather to Leith Hill's more southerly neighbour and the wide top of Pitch Hill. From excavations in 1930 proof was obtained of a hill camp on Holmbury Hill dating from 150 B.C. to 50 A.D. The camp is now rather overgrown with brambles and bracken but can be traced round the four sides of the top. This is a wonderful walk for any time of the year, but in winter the views are enhanced by the absence of leaves and undergrowth.

How to get there: By 23 or 25 bus from Guildford, 417 Sunday Ramblers bus then a 448 bus to Peaslake (Mon–Sat). By car to Peaslake turning off the A25 at Gomshall. The car park is down Pond Lane next to *The Hurtwood Inn*.

Walking back to the Inn we turn left, then right, then left again up Radnor Road opposite the War Memorial. Almost immediately there is a steep footpath on the left but if this looks too steep we can continue along the road and turn left along Plaws Hill which will bring us to the top of the steep footpath.

With Tor Cottage on our left we go forward on a well-defined path under trees, over various crossing tracks, down a dip and up the other side, soon bearing slightly right with a field on our left. At a fork we keep left with fields around a large house still on our

27

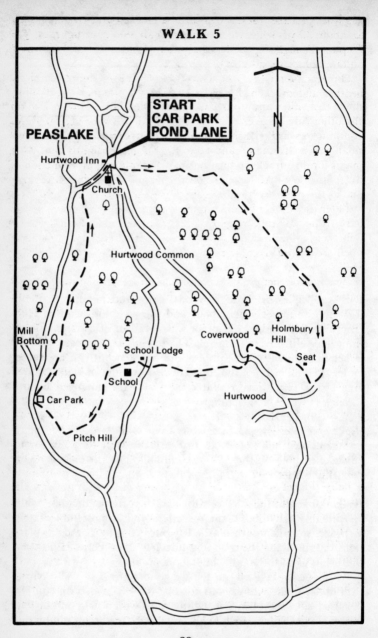

PEASLAKE

START CAR PARK POND LANE

Hurtwood Inn

Church

Hurtwood Common

Mill Bottom

School Lodge

Coverwood

Holmbury Hill

Seat

School

Hurtwood

Car Park

Pitch Hill

left. Just past the house we go over a crossing track and forward for about 30 yds when we turn right on another crossing track. We keep on through the conifers and after ignoring a track forking off on our right soon go uphill.

Our track is now very sandy and the vegetation mainly conifers, heather and bracken. Later we can see our track ahead dipping down to a valley and up the other side. We cross the valley and on the other side go over a crossing track at the top of the hill and continue forward on a small path. We go over a crossing track at a small green "triangle" and continue on going slightly left. At a major forestry track we turn right and are shortly at a junction of five paths. We take the third on the left, which is straight ahead, and as the path bears right again and forks we take the right fork.

Later the hillside becomes fairly open giving good views on our left. At the next fork we go left and continue round the hillside for a further half mile keeping to the main path. We finally reach the open space and circular memorial seat at the top of Holmbury Hill.

Leaving the memorial on our left we cross the open space to two paths. We take the left one, leading slightly downwards and continue round the edge of the hill, ignoring three paths which successively join us on our right. The path then bears right and at a T junction we turn left on to a main path and immediately take the right fork going downhill on a wide path to a line of concrete blocks preventing car access where we turn left along a broad track, bearing left to Hurtwood Control car park 1 on our right. We follow down to a narrow tarmac road where we turn right and after a few yards take a path on the left through trees, going slightly downhill.

We turn left on a crossing track and shortly turn right over a stile. A stile leads us to an enclosed path, which takes us across the valley giving pleasant views. When the path goes slightly uphill to a holly thicket we continue forward and are finally out on the road. We are now opposite the lodge of The Duke of Kent School and the public footpath goes through the school grounds. We take the drive into the school leaving the lodge on our right and when the drive turns left towards the main school building we take a smaller path on the right and proceed uphill on a grassy path under trees, leaving the sports field on our right. We bear left behind buildings uphill, then go through a gap in the perimeter fencing, and maintain direction over a crossing track. We come out on a well-defined track where we turn left, shortly encountering a fork where we turn right. After going uphill we turn left on a crossing track and eventually emerge into the open with panoramic views and the South Downs visible on a clear day. We continue on our path, keeping to the left on the edge of the hill top and finally turn right to the main open space of Coneyhurst, or Pitch Hill with O.S. trig point at a height of 843 ft. We continue beyond the trig point on a sandy track, going right at a fork, and soon left around fencing encircling a disused quarry. We can bear right around the quarry dropping down on various paths to the road, or continue on our path leaving the quarry on our right. In both cases we reach the road by a car parking space.

Without actually going out to the road we turn right through the car parking area and along the track known as Mill Bottom under the trees which are mainly beech. At a fork we keep left and continue on a pleasant and easy path in the same direction for over a mile until we reach Hurtwood Control car park 2 which leads out to the road. Here we turn right and, using a parallel path at a slightly higher level on the right of the road, continue into Peaslake passing the church and a small shop. *The Hurtwood Inn* is on our left and the car park behind it.

Refreshments: Peaslake Inn and village store. Peaslake Parlour for lunches and teas about 100 yards from the centre of the village on the Shere road.

WESTCOTT

**Broomy Down, Townhurst Wood,
The Rookery. $6\frac{3}{4}$ miles**

This is an interesting walk over heathland and through woodland
where deer abound. It affords delightful views across the valley
and is pleasant at any time of the year. Very little mud will be
encountered.

How to get there: There is a reasonably good bus service, Nos. 412,
Green Line 773 or T22 from Dorking to Westcott which is about 2
miles from the centre of Dorking. Cars can be parked in the side
road leading from *The Cricketers* up to Westcott Church.

From the triangular village green at Westcott we continue along
the main road for a few yards to *The Cricketers* where we turn left.
Just past the church and opposite the graveyard on the left we
take a wide path on the right leading us over a grass area in front
of a few houses. We cross a small drive leading to the houses and
go forward to the centre one of three paths. We maintain direction
slightly downhill. Our path becomes gully-like with orange-
coloured sandhills on the right and we are soon out to the main
road by the Rookery Lodge.
  We cross the main road turning left, continue past Balchins
Lane and turn right up Coast Hill Lane, which almost immediately
turns left while we continue forward on an enclosed footpath
between gardens. We are soon walking between wire fences in an

31

WALK 6

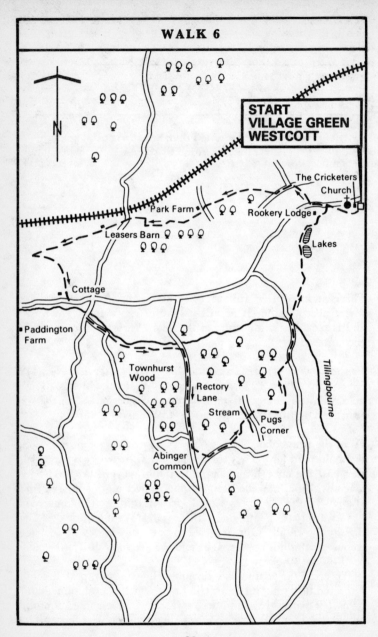

START
VILLAGE GREEN
WESTCOTT

The Cricketers
Church

Park Farm

Rookery Lodge

Leasers Barn

Lakes

Cottage

Paddington
Farm

Townhurst
Wood

Rectory
Lane

Stream

Pugs
Corner

Abinger
Common

Tillingbourne

area of holly, beech and conifer trees and after bearing left and slightly downhill we are out on a small tarmac drive. Here we turn left on to a farm track bounded by fields keeping right when it forks. We proceed through trees on a wide track, pass a red brick house and continue to Park Farm.

With the farm house on the right we go forward with farm buildings either side. We keep on this track with Deerleap Woods on the left and open fields on the right with pleasant views across the valley to White Downs. After about half a mile we are out in the road which leads from Effingham to the A25. We turn left and then almost immediately right on a well-defined path, later passing the Bishop Wilberforce monument, which marks the spot where he was thrown from his horse and killed in 1873, and Leasers Barn. After a while we cross a stile leading to an open field and keep left up to another stile leading into woodland. We go forward and uphill on a wide track for about 150 yards when we turn left on another wide track. Soon we have a clearing on our right at the end of which we go forward bearing slightly left into pine trees down to a stile and open field. We go forward leaving some isolated trees on our left then cross a stile to a path with the walled courtyard of the stable block of former Abinger Hall on our right. This pathway has been planted with bulbs for the enjoyment of walkers.

Our path comes out to the main road which we cross to a stile opposite and going diagonally across the field to a holly tree and stile we come out to a secondary road where we turn right and then shortly left into a smaller road. We pass Abinger Mill House on the left and go over a stile to a path into a wood with a stream on our left. We remain on this path through Townhurst Wood for over half a mile. Deer may be seen here if we are quiet. We continue over a stile into a road, Rectory Lane, where we turn right. We remain on this road for almost half a mile. About 150 yards past a turning on the right and just past some wooden gate posts at the side of the road we take a footpath on our left continuing forward over a crossing track keeping left when it forks. Our path bears left and is soon parallel with a small road on our right. At Mundies Farm track we join the road and then turn left down a private drive to Pugs Corner. The drive ends at a house where we turn right crossing a stream by a bridge and going over a stile to a small path opposite climbing steeply uphill. Shortly after the path flattens out we go over a stile into a wider track and almost immediately turn left and soon left again, still with the wire fence on our left. We continue along this pleasant grassy track and later turn right on a well-defined path which soon goes downhill, bears left and becomes parallel with a sunken road on our right.

We eventually come out over a stile to the road, where we turn left, and after crossing the Tillingbourne we turn right, going uphill into trees and emerging into a private drive. The footpath crosses the drive diagonally left up a steep bank, and through trees to a bridleway where we turn left towards a house.

We pass the house on our left, going through brick gate posts and turning right on a footpath to the left of a bridleway. At the end of the path we turn right, cross a wide track immediately turning left through wooden posts onto an enclosed path. This takes us steeply downhill to a wider bridleway where we maintain direction passing a lake on our right and going through the Rookery on the main drive past several delightful houses. We finally join the main road with the Rookery Lodge on our left. We turn right and take the footpath parallel with the road past the sandhills on our left. We keep forward on the main path crossing a drive and the open space in front of houses and finally out to the road by the graveyard where we turn left down the road to Westcott Church.

Refreshments: Inns and shops in Westcott

FRIDAY STREET

**Abinger Bottom, High Ashes,
Holmbury St Mary,
Pasture Wood and back to Friday Street.
$4\frac{1}{2}$ miles circular walk from
the Friday Street Car Park
but if done from Wotton Hatch Hotel
it adds another $2\frac{1}{2}$ miles,
making 7 miles in all**

This is a woodland walk for any time of the year, with bluebells and foxgloves in season and deer to be seen by the observant who keep quiet. There is very little mud even in winter and plenty of shade for a hot summer's day when it is advisable to take the hilly part of Pasture Wood at a very gentle pace. It is particularly beautiful on a sunny winter's day when the views are not obscured by trees in full leaf.

How to get there: By car to Friday Street. The car park is 200 yards west on the Abinger Road. Bus Nos. 412, Green Line 773 to Wotton Hatch.

Starting from the Friday Street Car Park
With the car park behind us and facing the road we turn right on to a narrow path parallel with the road, but at a higher level, following it to some wooden steps, which we go down turning left into the road and right to Friday Street lake.

From Wotton Hatch Hotel to Friday Street (just under $1\frac{1}{4}$ miles)

Leaving the hotel on our right we take the drive to a gate at the side of a wooden school building (yellow waymark), over a stile

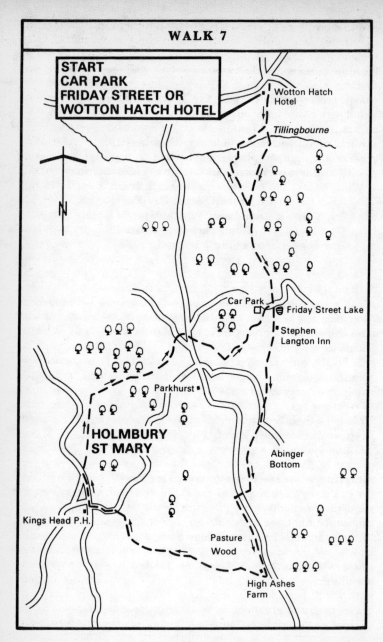

WALK 7

START
CAR PARK
FRIDAY STREET OR
WOTTON HATCH HOTEL

Wotton Hatch Hotel

Tillingbourne

N

Car Park

Friday Street Lake

Stephen Langton Inn

Parkhurst

HOLMBURY ST MARY

Abinger Bottom

Kings Head P.H.

Pasture Wood

High Ashes Farm

and diagonally right across a field to the corner. (N.B. *not* over a stile in the fence on the right.) We continue over another stile (yellow waymark), down through a strip of woodland and over a meadow crossing the Tillingbourne. Our path then takes us up towards a wood and over a stile, bearing right uphill through woods, crossing a wider track and keeping in the same direction uphill with a wire fence on the right, then downhill to ponds and a stream in the valley. We turn left at the T junction and go along this track for about half a mile, then over a stile by a bridge and pond on the right, keeping straight ahead on the wide bridleway, passing a couple of cottages, and out to the lake at Friday Street.

With the lake on our left we walk along the little road passing *The Stephen Langton Inn* and at the end of the lane we keep straight ahead on a footpath for about half a mile when it joins a tarmac lane. We turn left into Abinger Bottom and as the lane turns left we keep straight ahead on a path through open woods. When a fence appears on the left at a crossing track we turn right uphill to a small road where we turn left. Almost immediately there is a path on the right into trees leading to a well-defined bridleway on which we turn left parallel with the road with a field on our right. After nearly half a mile our track bears right downhill to join a farm drive where we turn right. As the drive bears right to High Ashes Farm we take the left downhill path inside the wood with a field on the right. Keeping straight ahead on the main path we ignore all side tracks. After nearly a mile we have a broken chestnut paling fence on our left and we continue downhill to a road.

We turn left at the road and down to the main road and Holmbury St Mary, where we turn right. For refreshment *The King's Head Inn* is along the first turning on the left.

To continue the walk we keep straight along the main road passing a bus shelter on the right and at an old village pump we turn right on a gravel drive, through a gate and straight ahead. At the fork just past the lodge we keep left, then straight on following the main track for nearly half a mile. Just before a gate we take the stile on the right and go steeply uphill through Pasture Woods. At the top the path levels out giving fine open views of the North Downs on the left. Keeping straight on and ignoring crossing tracks we go through open woods and finally down to a field ahead to cross a stile by a holly bush. We are now on an enclosed path which bears left out to a road. We cross straight over to a gravel path and are soon out to another road.

Here we turn right and after a few yards take a narrow path on the left into woods. We continue along this path and down to a wide sandy crossing track with a large sandy mound on the right. We cross this sandy track to a path opposite, bearing right. This path comes to a junction of several paths and we take the first on the left shortly keeping right at a fork and eventually out to a road.

For the car park we go up the wooden steps on the left and along the path which follows the road at a higher level.

If we are making for Wotton Hatch Hotel we turn right at the road to Friday Street lake and turn left into the bridleway along which we came. We keep along this for just over half a mile but instead of turning right on the path we used at the beginning of the walk we keep straight on. The track goes downhill and bears right to some crossing tracks which we cross continuing down with open fields on either side of the trees. We go over a stile and stream, then up a field ahead to a stile by the hedge. We turn right in the drive, and shortly over a stile in the fence on our right and across the meadow back to Wotton Hatch Hotel.

Refreshments: Holmbury St Mary. Stephen Langton Inn at Friday Street.

HORSLEY

Sheepleas. 5 miles

This is a pleasant walk at any time but makes a perfect autumn walk in country which compares with Burnham Beeches in Buckinghamshire for colour, the yellowing larches and dark green pines complementing the beech trees.

Walks 8 and 9 form a figure of eight and if a 10-mile walk is desired instead of turning left for the car park we cross the road to the signposted bridleway into Mountain Wood and follow Walk 9.

How to get there: By train to Horsley Station. By No. 408 Green bus to *The Duke of Wellington*, East Horsley. By car on the A246 from Dorking to Guildford turning left on the signposted road to Green Dene and Sheepleas half a mile east of East Horsley, continuing down the road for one and a half miles to the car park on the right.

If using 408 bus to *The Duke of Wellington*
Walk towards Guildford for about quarter of a mile and take the bridleway on the right to Place Farm and continue the walk from (A).

If starting from Horsley Station
We turn right down the approach road, crossing the main road to take the small road by the side of Horsley Hotel, keeping parallel

WALK 8

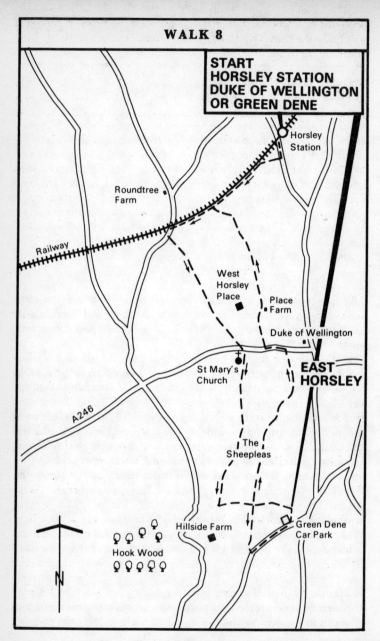

START
HORSLEY STATION
DUKE OF WELLINGTON
OR GREEN DENE

Horsley
Station

Roundtree
Farm

Railway

West
Horsley
Place

Place
Farm

Duke of Wellington

St Mary's
Church

EAST
HORSLEY

A246

The
Sheepleas

Hillside Farm

Green Dene
Car Park

Hook Wood

N

with the railway on our right. This soon becomes a footpath alongside the railway and eventually comes out into a road. Now continue the walk from (B).

Starting from the car park

We take a path at the right-hand corner of the car park and in a few yards turn right parallel with the road. Ignoring small crossing tracks in about a quarter of a mile we turn left on a wider crossing track. At the end of the avenue of yew trees we turn right and after about 200 yards we bear left to an open space by a path marker. We fork right to another path marker and turn right again, soon coming into an open space down which we walk to turn left on a crossing track and immediately right down to another open space. Our path enters woods and after going over a crossing track we continue to a T junction when we turn right into a woodland track with fields on our left and right. St Mary's Church, West Horsley, is soon visible in the distant trees on our left. When we come to the road we turn left and soon take a bridleway on the right to Place Farm.

(A) We follow the footpath signs through the farm into a fenced track, later hedged, and then across open fields eventually coming to the railway line. For return to the station we turn right.

(B) We turn left and follow the path alongside the railway line until it comes out into a road where we turn left and in a few yards, just past the 40 m.p.h. sign, we go over a stile in the hedge on our left. Keeping the hedge on our left we continue to a sign-post beside a stile and turn right round the next field to a stile in the hedge. Continuing with the hedge on our left we come out opposite St Mary's Church, West Horsley. Crossing the main road we take the bridleway with the church on our right.

This church is well worth a visit and much of it is very old. There is a fragment of Saxon stonework and late Norman pillars and arches; the tower doorway is also late Norman. A 12th century wall painting depicts St Christopher, the patron saint of travellers, and pilgrims' crosses can be seen on the arch of the 12th century north doorway.

When the bridleway enters woods we keep left through a barrier with trees on our right and an open area on our left. Our path continues through the centre of the next open area and we go through a barrier, turn right on a track and at once cross a junction of paths to another barrier giving access to an uphill path through another open area. This ends with a barrier after which we turn left, continue through an open area of beeches passing a path marker on the right, then keep left at the next fork and marker to an open space where we turn right. We soon turn right on a crossing path, keeping left when we merge into a wider track and maintaining direction with a field visible on our right. This path goes downhill and finally out to the road where we turn left for the car park. Alternatively, just before reaching the road we can turn left on a path which largely follows the line of the road and takes us back to the car park.

Refreshments: The Duke of Wellington on the A246.

MOUNTAIN WOOD

**and Netley Heath. 5 miles
A circular walk from the car park
in Green Dene through woodland**

This is a lovely walk for all seasons but is particularly recommended for the autumn when the larches of Mountain Wood are yellowing. In addition there are many different types of fungi to be seen and blackberries and sweet chestnuts for the gathering.

How to get there: By car on the A246 Leatherhead to Guildford, turning left on the signposted road to Green Dene and Sheepleas half a mile east of East Horsley, continuing down the road for a mile and a half to the car park on the right.

From the car park we turn right along the road for a short distance to a signposted bridleway on the left into Mountain Wood. We keep on the main track for about half a mile bearing left at the end of a cleared area on the right. We later drop steeply down to a wide forestry road where we turn right. At a fenced lumber area we turn left on a track through trees. After three quarters of a mile, in a more open area the track bears left but we maintain direction on a smaller path.

We finally turn right on a droveway, soon ignore a left turning and after a quarter of a mile turn left through posts to the open space of Hackhurst Downs. As we go forward to a view point on the right we ignore a left fork (acorn sign). Retracing our steps we

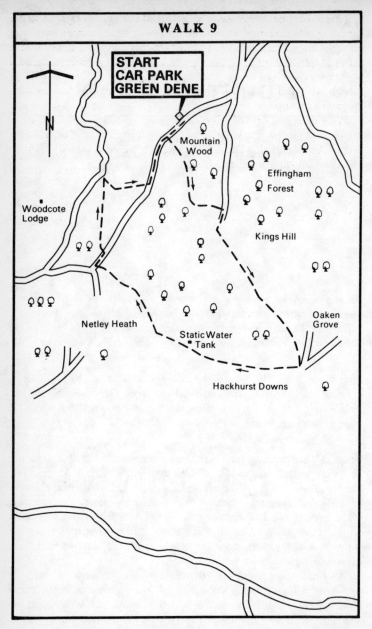

START
CAR PARK
GREEN DENE

Mountain
Wood

Effingham
Forest

Woodcote
Lodge

Kings Hill

Netley Heath

Oaken
Grove

Static Water
Tank

Hackhurst Downs

turn left on the droveway for about three quarters of a mile, ignoring side turnings. When the droveway bears left we continue straight ahead on a grass path later leading us into a wider track. After about 50 yards, just after a track turns off on the left, we take a path on our right down through trees and out to a tarmac drive which we cross to a path opposite, keeping on this for about a quarter of a mile to the road.

We turn right on the road for a short distance, then left on a signposted footpath taking the right-hand one of two paths. Later we are between fields and at a T junction we turn sharply right to the road and left for the car park.

RANMORE

Six Acre Copse, High Barn, Yew Tree Farm. Pigdon. 4½ miles

This is a varied walk of woods and fields in a little known area, with changing views. It is lovely in spring and autumn while the bare trees of winter open up the viewpoints still further. It may be somewhat muddy in wet weather.

How to get there: By car on the A24 from London turning off for Guildford just before Dorking Station (Ashcombe Road) but keeping straight on along the Ranmore Road instead of turning left for Guildford. Stoneyrock Road is the second turning on the right about 3 miles from Dorking Station, and there is a car park on the left just before reaching a cottage.

Just before the cottage we turn left on a signposted footpath starting on a wide track and in a few yards forking left on a parallel path which later rejoins the track. We continue between fields on a fenced path which is rather muddy during wet weather. After going down a dip with a house on the left we go up a drive to the road.

We cross the road to a gravelled drive ahead and as this bears right we cross a stile, maintaining our direction, then go over another stile and *straight* down the field to a road which we cross diagonally right to a footpath. We go up through a wood with fields on the right, over a couple of stiles and at the second stile

WALK 10

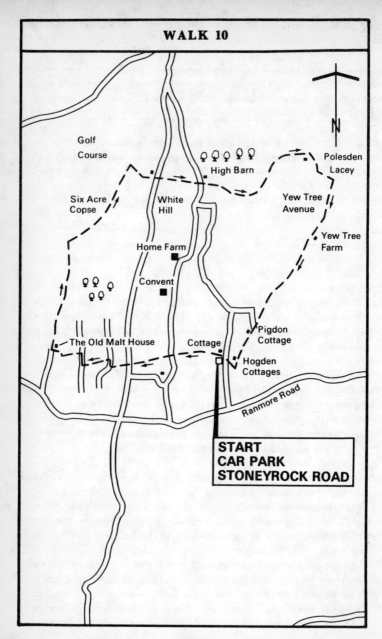

Golf Course

Six Acre Copse

White Hill

High Barn

Polesden Lacey

Yew Tree Avenue

Yew Tree Farm

Home Farm

Convent

Pigdon Cottage

The Old Malt House

Cottage

Hogden Cottages

Ranmore Road

**START
CAR PARK
STONEYROCK ROAD**

bear right to another stile and a footpath sign. We turn left with a wire fence on our left to a gate into a wide bridleway.

Here we turn right and very soon left over a signposted stile, down the side of a field, then through a wood to a beautiful timbered house, *The Old Malt House*, which we keep on our right, turning right into a bridleway. We follow the bridleway for about a quarter of a mile and at a house we turn right on a path. After about 200 yards we take a path forking off on the left through woods, following it for over half a mile, later with fields nearby on the right. After a rustic barrier we follow a wire fence on our right to a junction of paths where we take the right waymarked fork through Six Acre Copse, eventually coming out to a golf course.

Maintaining our direction, we cross the golf course to the left-hand end of a belt of trees round which we turn right. With an electricity hut on our right we cross another golf fairway to a grassy track with the grounds of a large house on our left, coming out to a road. Crossing the road we take a track opposite which leads us to another road and High Barn.

We cross to a drive opposite and continue on a path for a quarter of a mile on the edge of woods to a junction of paths. Here we turn left on a path through a narrow belt of trees, following it for half a mile. We finally have an open field on our right and at an old cattle trough on the right we cross a stile, go over a crossing track and bear right round a field towards buildings on the Polesden Lacey estate. At a drive we turn right to go under a thatched bridge, passing on our left the date (1861) marked in the flintstone embankment. When the drive turns left we continue ahead down a spectacular avenue of yew trees and when it joins another track we bear right passing Yew Tree Farm on our left and ignoring a path forking off to the right.

Soon after passing the farm we turn right into a field through a gate at the side of a large beech tree. We keep along the top edge of this field with the woods on our left and lovely views across the valley over to High Barn. At the end of the first field, after going through the remains of a hedge with a few isolated large trees, we bear diagonally right down a sloping field to a stile in a hedge which we cross bringing us into a track bounded by a flint wall.

Here we turn left and go straight ahead passing Pigdon on our right. At the next building, Hogden Cottages, we turn right uphill with the cottage gardens on our right and finally out to the road and the car park.

RANMORE AND POLESDEN LACEY

**From Boxhill Station through the woods of Ranmore
and Polesden Lacey. 6½ miles**

A zigzag walk in the lovely woods of Ranmore Common with
beech and oak trees, bluebells, foxgloves, orchids, and deer if you
are quiet. It is recommended for any time of the year.

How to get there: By train to Boxhill Station. There is a car park at
the station. Green bus 470 or Green Line Coach 714 to Burford
Bridge Hotel where there is a free car park.

Leaving Boxhill Station we go up the steps and turn left over the
bridge taking the left fork, Chapel Lane. We stay on the road for
half a mile but there is a parallel footpath on the left for some of
the way. Passing Burney Road and the last of the houses on our
left, we take a footpath diagonally left between wire fences across a
field to a T junction where we turn left. The remains of an ancient
chapel can be seen on the right. We continue along this tree-
fringed bridleway and just underneath the pylon lines we take a
right fork and after a few yards we go over a stile on the right,
keeping parallel with the telegraph wires to another stile. Keeping
along this path with a wire fence and open fields on our right and
a sloping wood on the left, we go over stiles and along a hedge on
our right to a cottage and a road. Here we turn left and after a
quarter of a mile we pass a cottage on the right, then an open field,
soon coming to a wood where we turn right uphill. At the top of

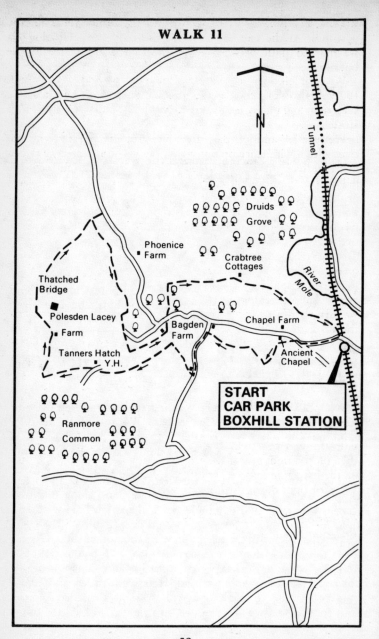

Druids Grove

Phoenice Farm

Crabtree Cottages

River Mole

Tunnel

Thatched Bridge

Polesden Lacey Farm

Bagden Farm

Chapel Farm

Tanners Hatch Y.H.

Ancient Chapel

START CAR PARK BOXHILL STATION

Ranmore Common

the hill at a junction of paths we turn right soon going slightly downhill. At the end of the wood the path turns left down a waymarked path between wire fences to a bridleway at the bottom.

We turn left on a field path and soon enter woods. After about 100 yards we fork right going uphill. Later, at another fork we keep right and finally bear right downhill to Tanners Hatch Youth Hostel.

We turn left and just past the hostel grounds we fork right into trees with a wire fence on our right. The wood gives way to open fields on the right beyond which Polesden Lacey can be seen. We follow this path uphill through woods, keeping forward to a bridleway and cottage where we turn right downhill, passing Polesden Farm buildings at the bottom, then uphill again along a tarmac drive. At the top we turn right with the drive, soon going under a small thatched bridge, and again turning right with the drive. We pass the entrance to Polesden Lacey on our right, the house and gardens of which are well worth a visit.

To continue the walk we follow the drive for another quarter of a mile and after going slightly uphill to a line of trees on our right we turn right on a bridleway. After about three quarters of a mile this turns right into woods (a minor track continues on) and soon bears left downhill. We go under a bridge and continue to the bottom of the hill where the bridleway bears right, while we turn left and cross a field on a well-defined path. With Bagden Farm on our left we turn left on a crossing track and are soon at the road.

We cross to a signposted bridleway opposite, soon going through a gate and uphill into woods. After quarter of a mile at the top of the hill, with a stile and open field on the left we turn right on a path through yew trees. Soon we have an open field on the left, then on the right giving us views of Ranmore Church, then open on the left again and we are out to Crabtree Cottages and a lane. We turn right down the lane for about a mile to Boxhill Station.

Refreshments: Polesden Lacey Tea Rooms in the summer. Canteen at Burford Bridge car park.

DORKING

Deepdene, Betchworth Golf Course,
Glory Wood. 6 miles

This is a pleasant walk in woods and over farmland keeping quite close to Dorking but giving us views of the hills we have walked in other walks in this book. A little mud will be encountered in winter but in April and May the larch woods near the Betchworth Golf Course are turning green and there are bluebells in the woods.

How to get there: By train or bus to Dorking Station where there is a car park.

From Dorking Station approach road we turn left into the main road and after going under the railway bridge we take the first turning on the right, following it to the main road where we cross to Moores Road. This soon forks and we keep right, going uphill to the open green of Cotmandene, forward towards four lime trees on the green and then down to Chart Lane, where we continue the same direction.
   This joins the main road which we cross bearing slightly left to a signposted footpath leading up to Deepdene. We are soon walking parallel with the main road among rhododendron thickets. When the track turns right we turn sharply left and still uphill with occasional wooden steps in the steepest parts. At the top we bear

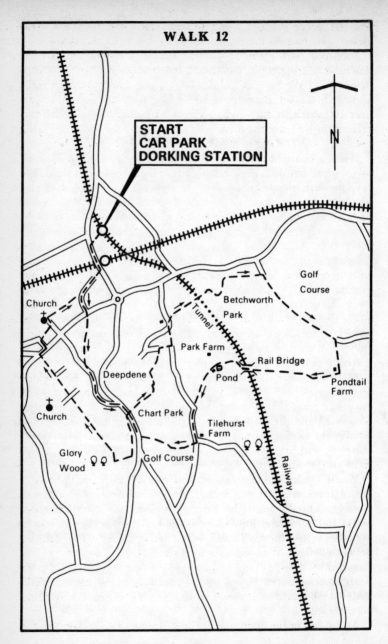

WALK 12

START
CAR PARK
DORKING STATION

N

Golf
Course

Church

Betchworth
Park

Tunnel

Park Farm

Rail Bridge

Deepdene

Pond

Pondtail
Farm

Church

Chart Park

Tilehurst
Farm

Glory
Wood

Golf Course

Railway

left and as we proceed along the now flat path there are good views to be had on the right over the golf course and beyond.

Soon our path leads us to a tarmac drive where we turn left downhill bearing right between houses and gardens of the Deep-dene estate. We turn right at a T junction, finally bearing right and out to a road, Punchbowl Lane, where we turn left. After just over 100 yards we turn right along a tarmac drive and when this turns right we leave the drive by a footpath on the left under larch trees.

When a boarded fence on the left of our path comes in sight we take a small footpath slightly uphill into the trees on our right. We keep forward along the top with the open space of the golf course on our right and good views on our left. Keeping to the higher path we eventually pass the rear of the Club House on our right and bear right over the drive to a white gate and track across the golf course. After about half a mile we turn right on a signposted footpath with a pond on our right, keeping to the edge of fields with hedge and ditchlike stream on our right and making for Pondtail Farm. We cross the farm track into a field, where after a few yards we turn right over a plank bridge and stile, going forward along the edge of a field with a small stream on our right. After bordering two fields we go over a stile into a narrow belt of young conifers, then turn right and immediately left again on a track at the edge of a field with a ditch and conifers on our left.

After about a quarter of a mile we go under a railway bridge and across a field on a wide grassy track leading towards Park Farm. The track takes us over a stile with pond and farm buildings on our left and the main farmhouse uphill on the right. We do not go over the cattle grid but turn left on another track with trees on our right and fields on our left. We proceed past a cottage on our right and downhill to a road where we turn left.

When Tilehurst Lane turns off on our left we turn right on a grassy track which leads across the golf course, uphill through woods and finally out to the main road, where we turn right. After about 150 yards and just before Chart Lane turns off we cross to the other side of the road and take a small doubling-back pathway between hedges. We soon have fields on our right and on our left, screened by trees, a deep drop down to the main road. Our path bears right into open woodland known as Glory Wood, and uphill under some spectacular beech trees giving a good view of Dorking on our right.

At the end of the open space on our right our path re-enters the woods and when it shortly forks we keep left and are soon at a seat where we turn right along the main track through Glory Wood. We continue downhill and out through a gate into a field with a seat on our left and fenced woods on our right.

We come out through school buildings and continue direction on a path between houses and gardens. After passing a flintstone wall on our left, we go down some steps, cross a road leading to a car park, downhill at the side of shops in Chequers Yard and out into the main street of Dorking.

Here we turn right, cross over, and at the sign 'Job Centre' turn left through the churchyard, bearing right, and out to a small road. We turn left past *The Malt House* and turn right into a park following the Pipp Brook out to a road where we turn left down to the main road. We turn left and go under the railway bridge and so back to Dorking Station.

Refreshments: In Dorking. Tea shops and inns.

LEITH HILL

**The eastern slopes of Leith Hill,
Redlands, Anstiebury Farm,
Kitlands. $5\frac{1}{2}$ miles**

This is an exhilarating walk with magnificent views on paths amid deer country, far from the throng of people. Concentration is necessary as we twist and turn among the heather and trees.

How to get there: By car from Dorking on the Coldharbour Road to a car park at the Landslip just south of Coldharbour village and just beyond the bend sign in the road. By bus or train to Holmwood Station.

The walk starts from the car park at the Landslip but if starting from Holmwood Station turn to (3).
    From the car park between the road on the left and a high slope on the right we go up a clear path around the steep hillside. Either fork will join a well-defined path coming up from the road where we turn right and uphill through conifers which later give way to beech trees. At the top, by a National Trust sign, *Mosses Wood*, on the right, we go through two wooden posts downhill through a wood on a main track which is joined by another from the right and proceeds to a crossing track with a deep gully on our left known as Cockshott Hollow. The main path on the left goes up to the tower at the top of Leith Hill but a more interesting path is the small one on the left following the edge of Cockshott Hollow and round the edge of the hill. This eventually joins the top of the main path.

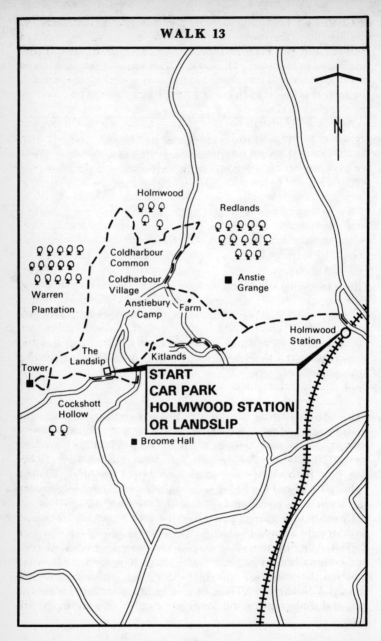

Holmwood

Redlands

Coldharbour
Common

Warren

Plantation

Coldharbour
Village

Anstiebury
Camp

Farm

Anstie
Grange

The
Landslip

Kitlands

Holmwood
Station

Tower

Cockshott
Hollow

**START
CAR PARK
HOLMWOOD STATION
OR LANDSLIP**

Broome Hall

The top of Leith Hill is 965ft but a height of 1000ft can be attained from the tower which was originally built by Richard Hull of Leith Hill Place in 1766. He died in 1772 and by his wish was buried in the tower. The tower fell into decay but was restored in 1795. At some later period a turret was added giving access to the roof. It is said that thirteen counties may be seen from the top on a very clear day.

We retrace our steps back to the top of Cockshott Hollow and cross over to the path with the National Trust sign, *Dukes Warren*. At a crossing track we turn left. This path loops back to the path we have just left but gives superior views. Rejoining the main path we turn left and in less than 100 yards where two paths turn off on the left we take the second left one with larch trees on the left.

We pass one crossing track and at the next we turn right on a wide sandy track. Later it joins a number of paths. We take the second on the left, a small uphill path through trees and after about 150 yards go through a cutting in a small bank at a junction of paths. Keeping straight ahead on a wide forestry track we eventually come out into a broad sandy track by a static water tank.

The walk can be shortened here by turning right along the wide track for nearly half a mile until it comes out at Coldharbour village where we turn right for just over half a mile to the car park, or if Holmwood Station is required we turn left to the road junction and continue at (1).

To continue the walk from the static water tank we turn left and at a junction of paths take a well-defined track downhill on the right. Crossing a wide forestry road we go down the path opposite to a crossing track with Lower Meridan Farm on the left where we turn right for about a quarter of a mile. We then turn left downhill through plantations and across a field making for the trees opposite. Our path crosses a small stream before we take the steep uphill path ahead through conifers, finally emerging on a forestry track where we continue direction to the road.

Crossing to a gate opposite into Redlands we take the small path straight ahead uphill with a broad track and a water tank on the left. At a direction stone at the top we turn right along a path and eventually come out to a road where we turn left. At the road junction the walk can be shortened by keeping straight ahead through Coldharbour Village and back to the car park. There is an inn, and confectionery and ice cream can be obtained in the village.

If Holmwood Station is required rejoin the walk here.

(1) At the road junction we turn left and shortly turn left along the fenced path to Anstiebury Farm. Just beyond the farm buildings we take a stile on the right and go across a field to the far corner where there is another stile leading into woods. The path goes downhill, soon with a wire fence on our left, down to another stile and out into a field. We cross the field slightly left to a stile by a large oak tree, then keep along the hedge on our left and over a final stile into a lane.

For Holmwood Station we turn left and continue back the way we came, going through the kissing gate into the enclosed path which brings us back to the road and bus stop.

To continue the walk back to the Landslip, after crossing the stile into the lane we turn right and follow the lane until it comes out to a road in which we turn right passing the lodge of Kitlands on the left.

(2) Just before a house on the right we turn left over a stile. Passing under telegraph wires, we keep along the edge of a field with the hedge on the right, over another stile and out to a lane where we turn right. Ignoring left forks we continue forward and later with a wall on our left we take a left fork. Keeping on this tarmac drive we go through an avenue of cypress trees and out to a road where we turn left, noticing fine views on the left before the road becomes treelined. After about 100 yards at a point where the broken fence on the right ends and opposite a signposted stile on the left we turn right by a post and a large beech tree, then straight uphill through beech trees, where the path becomes more easily discernible. Eventually the path leads us out to a road and through posts where we turn left to the car park on our right.

(3) If starting from Holmwood Station we walk back a short distance towards Dorking and at the last house on the left and at the 30 m.p.h. sign we turn left through a kissing gate along an enclosed path out to a lane where we turn left. After just over quarter of a mile we take the middle one of three tracks. We follow this for nearly half a mile, finally bearing right out to the road where we turn right, soon passing the lodge of Kitlands on the left. Now continue at (2).

Refreshments: Available from the top of Leith Hill most weekends and fine days.

HEADLEY HEATH

Mickleham Downs. 5 miles

Here are two walks from the car park on Headley Heath, the first walking over the Heath and Mickleham Downs, mostly on National Trust land, the other (Walk 15) over fields to Headley Church, returning over the Heath. Both walks are pleasant, with bluebells in April and May. Both walks are recommended for any time of the year.

How to get there: By bus No. 416 from Leatherhead Post Office, approximately an hourly service with no service on Sunday. By car on the B2033.

At the mobile canteen by the car park with the road behind us we go forward over an open space, cross a main horse track and continue on a wide path soon with a silver birch wood on the right and open heath on the left. We are shortly at a junction of paths where we maintain direction by taking the third path from the left going slightly downhill. At a wide junction of 5 or 6 paths we continue on a broad track still with woods on our right. Later our path goes through a more open area dropping gradually downhill and after crossing a track bears left into trees. We then turn left with a wire fence on our right noticing good views of White Hill across the valley. The path clings to a steeply sloping hillside following National Trust boundary posts on our right and then

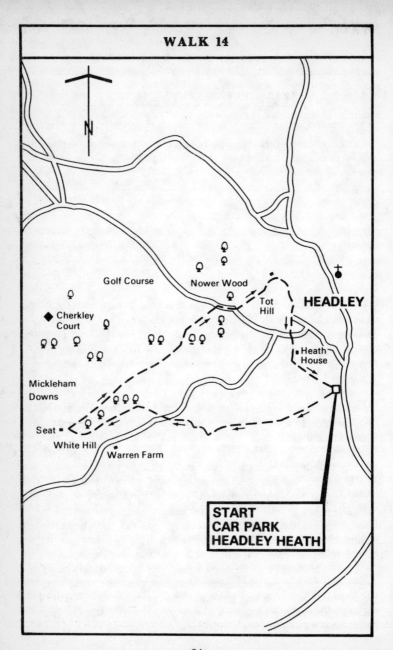

Golf Course

Nower Wood

Tot Hill

HEADLEY

Cherkley Court

Heath House

Mickleham Downs

Seat ■

White Hill

Warren Farm

START
CAR PARK
HEADLEY HEATH

goes steeply down to the edge of the wood with a field on our right.

Coming out of the woods into open heath we turn right on a small path beside a main bridleway. In 30 yards or so, we turn sharply right into trees and go up a steep path. At the top of the hill we turn right with the boundary wall of Wentworth Hall on our left. This path bears right and downhill eventually coming out to a road, Lodgebottom Road, with a cottage on the left.

Crossing the road to a footpath opposite we take the lower path at first parallel with the road. After about 300 yards at a junction of several paths and where our main path bears right, we keep straight ahead uphill under yew trees, ignoring the left fork with posts across. The woods here are a mixture of very fine beech trees and yews with an underplanting of box. After a further half a mile we emerge into open scrubland with a seat on the right and fine views of the north slopes of Boxhill. We turn right just before the seat, following a fence on the left as it turns left but soon leaving it to turn right. After perhaps 60 yards a path on the left runs rather indistinctly between two beech trees, the right one of which leans heavily to the right. We take this path with open beech woods on the right and, at first, scrubby wood on the left. We bear slightly left with the path emerging on to the open space at the top of Mickle-ham Downs. We turn right and continue for more than half a mile along this splendid grassy ride with lovely beech trees on the right.

At the end of the ride we enter the woods by a National Trust sign keeping along the fenced path with Surrey Naturalist Trust Nature Reserve on our right and later with open views of Headley Heath, eventually coming out through posts to a road. Here we turn right and at the end of the wood on our left take a bridleway on the left. Very soon we go over a stile on the right into a field with a wood on our left bearing left round the edge of the wood. When the wood turns sharply left we keep straight on to a stile ahead, down a field with wire fencing on the left, over another stile, passing a house on the left, and over another stile in the left-hand corner into a lane, in which we turn right. The lane comes to a road and we again turn right passing a farm on the right. We keep straight on ignoring a left fork.

We are soon at a major road which we cross to the National Trust sign and take the left-hand one of two paths, uphill. Soon the path forks and we go left continuing on through bracken until we have the thick holly hedge of Heath House on our left. As the hedge ends we cross a small tarmac drive and continue on a grassy path maintaining the same direction. Our path soon brings us out to a small open space with several paths turning off. We are now very close to the car park and if we maintain direction on any path we will soon be in sight of the car park and mobile canteen.

Refreshments available from the mobile canteen at Headley Heath car park.

HEADLEY AND HEADLEY HEATH

5 miles

This walk includes some field walking but is mainly in the woods and heathland of Headley Heath. Those familiar with this popular National Trust area may well find their knowledge pleasantly extended. An alternative ending to the walk is given for those who would prefer to avoid a fairly steep descent and corresponding ascent.

This walk starts from the main Headley Heath car park opposite the cricket ground. With our backs to the road we leave by the right-hand corner of the car park, turning right, parallel with the road. We soon fork right and at the road junction cross to a signpost, then turn left parallel with the road. After the path becomes surfaced we turn right down a gravel drive, then left on a footpath with a house on the right. At a footpath sign we turn left over a field to a stile and maintain direction over various stiles till we reach Headley Church. We turn left through the churchyard and reach the road with *The Cock* on our left, crossing diagonally left to the bus stop.

Here we turn right on a surfaced path which soon gives pleasant views. Reaching the road, we turn right, keeping right at a road junction. Almost at once we turn left along the left-hand edge of a National Trust open space, Tot Hill, soon entering woods and following the path downhill to a small road where we turn left. We

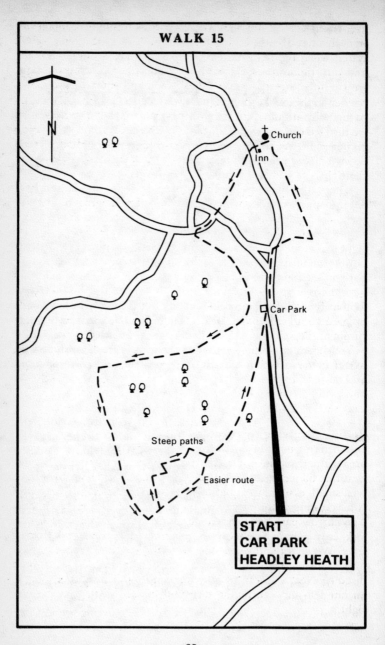

WALK 15

Church

Inn

Car Park

Steep paths

Easier route

START
CAR PARK
HEADLEY HEATH

68

are soon at a road junction where we cross to the National Trust sign Headley Heath, taking the left-hand footpath going uphill. Later, when the path flattens, we pass a holly hedge on our left and turn right on a surfaced drive. At a large house on the right we continue direction on a sandy track and shortly go under a barrier on the left, keeping right down an open area over a crossing path and continuing down another open area at the end of which we turn left down a well-defined path with a seat some yards away on our right. We shortly go over a crossing track, and after going down a dip we keep right on a crossing track with fenced woods on the right.

Later, after the fence on the right ends, we go uphill and bear left into an open area, turning right along a wide grass path along the top of a ridge with splendid views. Meeting a crossing path, we turn left and follow the path to the open hillside, where we fork right to a rustic barrier and go downhill on a stepped path. At the bottom we turn right on a main bridleway, using a mud avoidance path on the right which shortly rejoins. As the bridleway begins to go uphill we go under a barrier on the left to a pleasant grassy footpath which later gradually gains height. After about half a mile we go under a barrier and turn left up a track, ignoring side turnings.

We shortly reach an open space with a junction of five paths and take the second on the left. A major path joins in on the right and on reaching an open area we turn right and soon right again on a wide green track.

Ending involving fairly steep path
Just before woods begin we turn left along the edge of an open area with trees on our right. We bear left with the path and continue till just before a clump of trees ahead, then we turn right on a small, easily missed path which twists downhill fairly steeply. After crossing a stony track we keep right at a fork and go uphill. The narrow path widens as it climbs uphill, and we keep left at a fork, cross a main bridleway and maintain direction uphill among trees. We continue over a stony crossing track, and shortly at a major crossing track at the top of the hill we turn left for a short distance. Near a seat in trees on our right we turn right, passing it on our left and continuing direction initially with trees on our right.

Alternative ending with less gradient

We continue on this wide green track to a major junction of paths and take the second on the left, later going down and uphill, ignoring side turnings. Eventually we reach a main crossing bridleway, turn left for a few yards with rustic barriers on our right, then bear left on a grassy track. After going through a small open area we are soon at a large open area where we turn right on a small path. This shortly brings us to a main crossing track on which we turn left for about 200 yards. We now turn right over grass to pass on our left a seat set among trees and continue direction initially with trees on our right.

Both alternatives now follow the same route

We are now on a wide grassy path and continue over a crossing grass path, then bear left, later keeping right at a fork. After one more minor crossing path we turn left on the next crossing path in an area of silver birches. Eventually, on reaching an open area with a junction of several paths, we bear left with the Jubilee Plantation and seat on our right and are shortly at the car park.

Refreshments: The Cock at Headley and the mobile canteen at the car park.

BOXHILL

**(i) Boxhill, Duke's Plantation, Juniper Top. $5\frac{3}{4}$ miles
(ii) Boxhill, Brockham Hills,
The Whites. 6 miles**

The two different endings can be interchanged thus giving a short walk of $4\frac{1}{4}$ miles or a rather strenuous but rewarding walk of $7\frac{1}{2}$ miles.

These two walks will greatly increase our appreciation of the beauty of the Boxhill area. They are suitable for any time of the year but will give most pleasure in early summer when the chalk downland flowers and butterflies abound, or in the autumn when we can enjoy the changing colours of trees and shrubs. The longer walk takes us steeply uphill and downhill several times but it is an exciting walk and well worth the effort involved. It could be considered a good training course for anyone contemplating a walking holiday! It is not advisable to do it just after rain as the chalk slopes are slippery when wet.

How to get there: By Green Line Bus 714 to Burford Bridge Hotel. By train to Boxhill Station. By car to the car park at Burford Bridge Hotel (one mile north of Dorking on the A24).

For both walks
From the station. Leaving Boxhill Station we turn right down the road to the main road, crossing by the subway, turning left and at the subway sign taking a small path on our right over a stile.

From the car park and Burford Bridge Hotel we walk towards

WALK 16

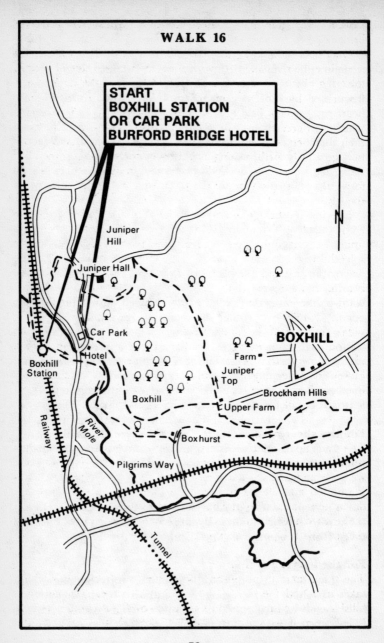

72

Dorking along the main road to the subway, just over the river bridge.

Once over the stile a grassy track takes us to the River Mole and we follow the riverside path with the steep wooded side of Boxhill towering above us. This is a beautiful stretch of the river, much frequented by fishermen of all ages. After some time our path bears right over a field and we cross the river by an iron bridge which was erected by The Ramblers Association in memory of their members who fell in the 1939–45 war. As an alternative we may go a little further along and cross by the stepping stones, but these are sometimes flooded. From the stepping stones we go forward a short distance till the path from the bridge joins in on the left.

Leaving the bridge we take the forward path away from the river and at a T junction in about 100 yards we turn left and uphill bearing right. As we mount steeply upwards we can see splendid views on our right and it is useful to look out for painted waymarks on trees. We keep upwards on a very steep path soon bearing right. As the path flattens, at an acorn sign, we go forward on the lower right-hand path till we finally emerge into the open.

We continue in the same direction on a small path around the contour of Boxhill with trees on our right and good views. In the summer this chalky downland area abounds in wild flowers and butterflies. Our path eventually bears right down a rough tree-lined track to a drive on which we turn left uphill, soon taking a footpath parallel with the drive. Later we turn right on a track.

For the shorter version
The track takes us uphill and bears right as a bridleway taking us round the side of the hill. After about a mile on this pleasant track we go round a sharp hairpin bend in an area known as Duke's Plantation and after a quarter of a mile at a gate we turn left down steps and shortly right at an acorn sign. We continue round the wooded hillside and at a crossing path turn right, soon reaching the road with Upper Farm Tea Gardens on our right.

For the longer version
The track takes us uphill and bears right as a bridleway which takes us round the side of the hill for half a mile. As the open hillside ends we turn right on a steep downhill path under yews. It is less steep if we go diagonally left through the yews. At the

73

bottom of the slope we turn left along a wide path with a fringe of yews and open fields with a view of Brockham on our right.

Ignoring crossing tracks we continue direction, passing an old war-time pill box on our right. This path leads us to a clearing which we cross with disused lime kilns on our left and some buildings on our right. After a stile we continue with a wire fence on our right. Avoiding branching paths we soon have open fields visible through the fringe of trees on our right. Just past a stile into a field on our right we fork left and soon go steeply uphill keeping on the main path until we reach a major chalky crossing track where we turn left gently uphill. Higher up, walking at the top of the left hand bank gives the best views.

Just before the top, by an acorn sign we turn left up steps to visit a gravestone on our right inscribed " 'Quick'. 26.9.36 to 22.10.44. An English thoroughbred". We continue past the grave on our right on a small footpath with a caravan site on our right and after a while our path joins a bridleway in which we turn left.

This track soon goes steeply downhill giving some fine views on our left through the trees. Later we turn right up some steps by an acorn sign and follow an uphill path with a handrail soon coming out on the bridleway through Duke's Plantation, at the hairpin bend. We take the right and slightly uphill arm and continue along it for a quarter of a mile. At a gate we turn left down steps and shortly right at an acorn sign. We continue round the wooded hillside and at a crossing path turn right, soon reaching the road with Tea Gardens on our right.

For both walks we have a choice of two ways back to Burford Bridge Hotel

(a) *Over "The Whites"* $1\frac{1}{2}$ *miles*

From Upper Farm Tea Gardens we turn left on the road for a few yards to a National Trust sign where we turn left on a small path into trees, soon bearing right on a path parallel with the road and following the acorn signs (North Downs Way). We later continue along the open hillside with a fringe of trees on our right. Opposite an open area on the other side of the road we bear left into trees soon turning right on a clear path leading to the memorial viewpoint on Boxhill. From this we bear right to the road where we continue for about 150 yards. Just past the National Trust Information Centre and Tea Gardens we turn left with fencing on our left. When this path forks it does not matter which fork we take, one goes past old fortifications and they both come out to the well-known white chalk track over the top of Boxhill. Noticing the views of Ranmore Common and Ranmore Church spire ahead, we go downhill on the ridge towards a red tiled house, and nearing the foot of the hill we bear left to the car park and Burford Bridge Hotel.

(b) *Over Juniper Top to Boxhill Station 3 miles*
Crossing the road diagonally left we go forward with the boundary fence of the caravan site on our right, later turning right with the fence. We soon take a path turning off on the left and follow it for about half a mile, ignoring side turnings. After crossing a major crossing track, at a National Trust sign, we ignore a left turning and maintain direction on a grassy path. We finally cross a stile into the open space of Juniper Top, with fine views of Mickleham Downs straight ahead and Ranmore Common in the distance. We keep to the open space in the centre of this shoulder of hill and go downhill on a gradual slope, with thick trees, mostly yews, on our left, and later birch trees. Continuing down the shoulder of the hill at the bottom the path enters a wooded area and we come out through a kissing-gate into Juniper Bottom, where we turn left, doubling back along the valley. On our right we have a field behind trees, and then a small wooded area. Just before an open slope we take a narrow path into woods. This is *not* the path outside the wood with the open space on the left.

Alternatively from Juniper Top it is possible to take a short cut down to Juniper Bottom and save about a quarter of a mile. Soon after yew trees on the left give way to silver birches, we leave the broad green centre track at a seat and take a narrow path on the left which winds down to Juniper Bottom by the wood and open space.

The path in the woods goes steeply uphill and at the top we ignore a left turning. Our track bears right, passes a house, Pinehurst, in trees on our left and finally winds down to the road which we cross to some steps opposite. These lead to a path parallel with the road which we rejoin after about a quarter of a mile. We continue direction for about 30 yards along the road then turn left on an enclosed footpath which later bears right downhill. After going down some steps and through a kissing gate we go forward along the edge of a field with the hedge on our left. This path later becomes enclosed and we cross a stile and a drive to an enclosed footpath at the side of a bungalow. We follow this down to the main A24 road, which we cross with care, taking a path immediately opposite.

This leads us under a railway bridge, where we bear left and go over a bridge crossing the River Mole, continuing on a grassy path with the railway embankment on our left. A stile takes us to an enclosed path leading to the road where we turn left to Boxhill Station a few yards away, or continue down the road to the main road and Burford Bridge Hotel.

Refreshments: The tea rooms at Upper Farm or National Trust Tea Rooms at the top of Boxhill.

REIGATE HILL

Reigate Hill, Colley Hill
4½ or 6¾ miles

In this walk we explore the breezy slopes of Reigate and Colley Hill with wide panoramic views, continuing along Juniper Hill, Buckland Hills and Lady Hill and returning along the ancient trackway at the foot of the range of hills. While being enjoyable at any season, this walk is particularly beautiful in autumn when the beeches at the foot of Colley Hill are changing colour. After winter rains, the lower paths become rather muddy in places and the steep path down through the Buckland Hills, for the shorter walk, should be avoided in rainy conditions.

How to get there: By Green Line bus No. 727 or Green No. 406 bus to the top of Reigate Hill. By car to car park at the top of Reigate Hill on A217.

From the car park we make for the footbridge over the main road, passing the refreshment hut and toilets on our right. We follow this tree-lined track for about three quarters of a mile, passing a water tower on our right, and coming out at the open top and non-functional memorial fountain of Colley Hill.
    Noticing the slopes of Leith Hill in the distance we continue along this grassy hill top through sundry clumps of hawthorn and yew and eventually come to a National Trust sign, *Colley Hill*. Keeping in the same direction along the hill top path, between a

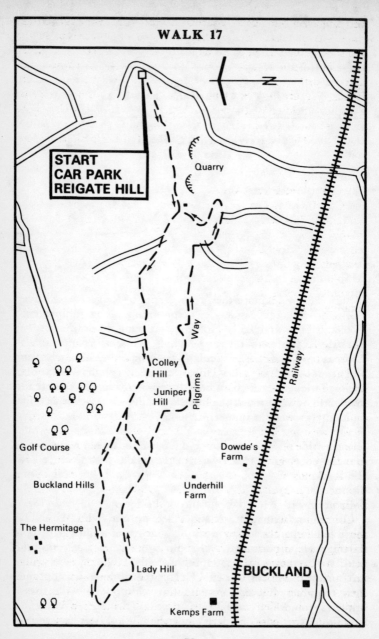

START
CAR PARK
REIGATE HILL

Quarry

Way

Pilgrims

Colley
Hill

Juniper
Hill

Golf Course

Buckland Hills

Dowde's
Farm

Underhill
Farm

The Hermitage

Railway

Lady Hill

BUCKLAND

Kemps Farm

wire fence on our left and shrubs on the right, we pass through three sets of posts, keeping left and ignoring branching paths. We soon come out on to a small tarmac drive where we turn left and right again almost at once on a path next to an iron gate marked with the names of two houses and a sign saying *Strictly Private*. We are now walking along the top of Juniper Hill on a rather enclosed path but in winter and spring giving good views on the left from time to time. Emerging at a house named Conybury Heights, we have the choice of either a short or long walk.

For the shorter version
By Conybury Heights is a "squeeze" leading into a narrow footpath with a holly hedge on the right and wire fence on the left, taking us down through the Buckland Hills. At the end of the fence we go through yews and soon very steeply downhill, coming suddenly out into the open with wonderful views. We continue downhill towards a clump of trees and just before the bottom turn left on a crossing track which is part of the ancient trackway running along the foot of this range of hills.

For the longer version
At Conybury Heights we continue forward in the same direction and are soon walking on the top of the Buckland Hills, still on an enclosed path, with the back of an occasional house on the left and open fields visible through the fringe of trees on our right. The path enters a wooded area which is undoubtedly muddy in winter or wet weather, but there are occasional paths avoiding the mud on either side of the main track, which soon bears left and emerges into the open, giving fine views of the Betchworth Clump, with the Redlands Heights and the side slopes of Leith Hill in the distance. On a clear day the South Downs are visible on the horizon.

Continuing with a fenced wood on our right, the path soon turns left for a short way downhill and then right again, thus skirting a rectangular field by turning right up the third side of the field. We are now on Lady Hill. Our path leaves the rectangular field and bears left into woods, soon going uphill for a short distance then resuming direction. Eventually our track meets a major bridleway on which we turn left downhill with steep banks on either side. Our path, bordered by ancient yews, bears left, giving good views on our right and sometimes glimpses of a white chalk cliff on our left.

At the point where a line of pylons in the open field on our right is very close to our path, at a North Downs Way sign we turn left on a rising path. This leads round the base of the hills over which we have walked and gives good views. Soon we are walking on an open path through an area noted in summer for its variety of wild flowers and butterflies.

We continue forward at the foot of the hills, sometimes in the open and sometimes under trees. We ignore a path forking right to Underhill Farm and very soon we are joined by a path on the left coming down from the Buckland Hills.

Both walks now follow the same route:
Later, having walked round the foot of Juniper Hill, we continue over a crossing track and go through a barrier to a yew-lined track following the path which twists and turns around the foot of Colley Hill.

At Colley Pits we ignore a fork on our left and go down some steps, still keeping along the foot of the hill ignoring all turnings off to the right. We finally come out into a tarmac road and go under a wooden barrier still maintaining our direction. In about 100 yards as the road turns right we fork left to a house, "Under-beeches", and turn sharply left again with a beech hedge on the left and wall on the right. This path soon becomes rutted and chalky, giving views on the left. We continue uphill to a granite memorial obelisk and when the track levels out we turn right up some steps which bring us back to the memorial fountain on Colley Hill which we passed earlier. Turning right we retrace our steps along the bridleway back to the car park.

Refreshments: The canteen in the car park at the top of Reigate Hill.

CHIPSTEAD VALLEY

Chipstead Valley and Long Plantation
$4\frac{1}{2}$ miles

This walk is in a delightful area very close to London with wild flowers on the hillside and good views across the valley.

How to get there: By train to Chipstead Station, going down Station Approach, turning left in the main road and right down Lower Park Road to the car park on the left. By bus Nos. 166 or 12a on Sundays to Chipstead Valley, alighting at *The Midday Sun*, walking along the road signposted to Banstead and turning right down Lower Park Road. By car to the Banstead Woods car park at the end of Holly Lane B2219.

We leave the car park by a kissing gate with toilets on our left and take an uphill path on the *outside* of Banstead Woods. We remain on this path for about a mile, without entering the woods, enjoying good views.

Later we are on open hillside with a field on our right and a fringe of trees and downward slope on our left. As the field on the right ends, our path turns left by a large beech tree and we go forward a few yards to a seat and a junction of three paths. We take the path on the extreme right with fine views across the valley on our left. Shortly our path enters an open beech wood but we double back on a small path on the left going down the hillside and over a crossing track. This is a small deviation to enjoy really

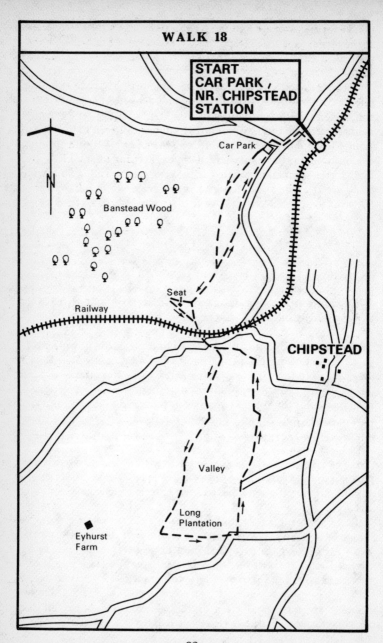

WALK 18

START
CAR PARK ,
NR. CHIPSTEAD
STATION

Car Park

N

Banstead Wood

Seat

Railway

CHIPSTEAD

Valley

Long
Plantation

Eyhurst
Farm

fine views and we soon join the path which was on the extreme left at the recent junction of three paths. We continue downhill across the railway and are soon out to the road which we cross bearing slightly left to a stile.

We go forward with a garden fence on our right but as the fence turns a corner we maintain direction and bear right up a slope to a stile which takes us through a narrow strip of woods and out to a field. We bear right uphill round the edge of this field to a stile into Long Plantation. Crossing the stile we turn left on a path through woods for about three quarters of a mile, keeping left at a fork and finally at a T junction turning left. We cross the valley on a wide track up to a stile and a road where we continue uphill for about 50 yards to another footpath on the left which leads us back along the other side of the valley.

When our path is joined by a track coming in on the right we continue in a forward direction with woods on our right and open valley on our left. When we have practically completed our return on the other side of the valley, we cross a stile at the side of a gate, maintain direction across an open field till we are opposite a stile on our right, then turn left downhill on a footpath which leads us back to the stile and road which we crossed earlier.

We now retrace our steps, crossing the railway and continuing straight up the uphill path, ignoring a path on the left, to the seat at the top where we turn right with a field on our left and hedgerow on our right. We shortly turn right on a crossing track, immediately taking a small path on the left. Enjoying good views ahead, we go forward with trees on our left, gradually losing height. The last part of this path is parallel with the road, a short distance away on our right, and we finally go through a rustic barrier to the car park on our left.

Refreshments and toilet facilities available at the car park.

COULSDON

Coulsdon, Happy Valley and Chaldon
5 miles (or alternatively 3¼ miles from the
Tea Rooms)

This is a lovely area very close to London where wild flowers
abound and through careful clearing many rarer plants are beginning to appear on the chalky slopes in the valley. The woods are a
beautiful sight in May with bluebells, red campion and white
stitchwort.

How to get there: By bus No. 190 to Downs Road, Coulsdon. Cars
may be parked a short distance up the road over Farthing Downs
or alternatively at the top of the Downs by the Tea Rooms.

There are many tracks going south over Farthing Downs and a
small tarmac road for cars. For the best views and to avoid the
sight of cars we keep to the side slopes well over to the right where
the Downs Road houses are partly screened by a fringe of yew
trees. As Westwood Road joins Downs Road we turn left up a
grassy track which leads uphill to the highest part of Farthing
Downs where there are two trees, a signpost and a seat. Here we
turn right along a well-kept wide grassy track on the top of the
Downs. Later the area known as Happy Valley can be seen ahead
on the left and we are well within sight of the Tea Rooms when at
white posts on the right we turn left on a bridleway. We continue
across the road and down the shoulder of the Downs bearing right
into a wooded area. Crossing another bridleway we maintain our

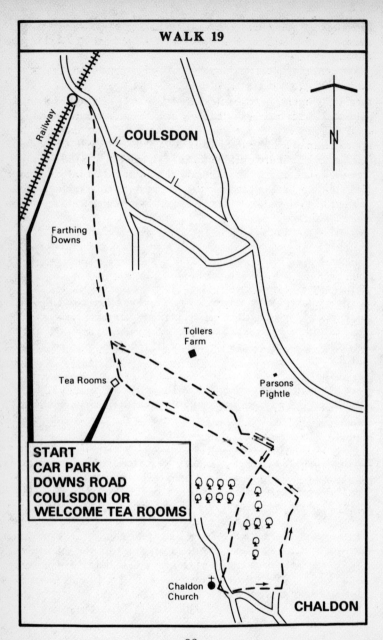

Railway

COULSDON

Farthing
Downs

Tollers
Farm

Tea Rooms

Parsons
Pightle

**START
CAR PARK
DOWNS ROAD
COULSDON OR
WELCOME TEA ROOMS**

Chaldon
Church

CHALDON

N

direction by going under a wooden bar and proceeding on a narrow path which takes us downhill through a small wood and out into the open.

We continue forward along the valley bottom for about half a mile enjoying good views. At a hedge which spans the valley we turn right uphill, over a stile, through a strip of woodland and over open fields on a well-defined track. Eventually we reach the road where we turn left and right almost at once on a small approach road leading to St Peter & St Paul's Church, Chaldon.

This ancient church, which dates back to 1100, contains many treasures, such as a tomb 600 years old, and a tablet inscribed in 1562, but chief among these is the unique and remarkable mural painted in 1170 but only discovered in 1870 under a preserving coat of whitewash.

Leaving the church by the other approach road on the right we go down to the road which we cross to a signposted footpath on a track with open fields on the left and backs of houses on the right. Soon we have a wood on our left and on reaching a crossing lane we turn left with the wood still on our left and houses and gardens on the right. At the last house the lane becomes a footpath and enters the wood sloping slightly downhill for about quarter of a mile until the valley becomes visible on our left.

Here we leave our track which continues downhill while we go through the hedge turning left along the open hillside with woods on our left. We are soon back at the hedge which spans the valley and we pass through a gap keeping up on the hillside with woods on our left and the valley bottom on our right. Our path takes us through a small wooded strip and out into the open again and we maintain direction. We re-enter the woods and our wide track soon leads us out to the Tea Rooms and toilets on our left. After refreshment we retrace our steps along Farthing Downs back to the car park and bus stop at Downs Road.

Refreshments: Tea Rooms at the top of Farthing Downs.

Chelsham

**Chelsham, Woldingham and back
$6\frac{3}{4}$ miles**

This is a pleasant summer walk with plenty of chalkland flowers
and butterflies on the downs and the field footpaths. Some mud
will be encountered in places more especially in the wetter
months.

How to get there: By Green 403 or 23 bus to Chelsham bus garage.
There is ample car parking space nearby.

We leave Chelsham bus garage and turn right along High Lane
just past *The Hare and Hounds*, shortly turning right along Plantation Lane and continuing on the main track with the valley
down on the left. After just over half a mile we take the first stile
on the left near a farm down in the valley and go straight across
the field to another stile in the fence. Keeping straight ahead we
make for another stile to the right of trees ahead. Crossing the
road to a stile opposite we go straight up the hill to a stile under
trees, through a strip of wood and out to a small residential road.
Here we turn left and as the road turns left we go straight ahead
on a footpath between beech and privet hedges, crossing another
small road, continuing forward, then down a stepped path to a
signposted footpath. We bear left along this for about half a mile
with occasional seats, woods on our left and a valley on our right
with good views. The last part of the path is fenced and eventually

89

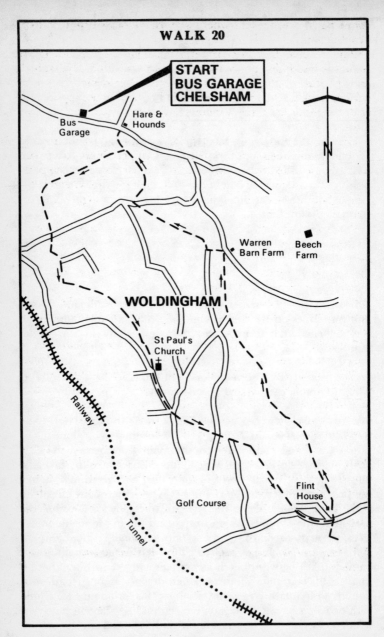

START
BUS GARAGE
CHELSHAM

Bus Garage

Hare & Hounds

N

Warren Barn Farm

Beech Farm

WOLDINGHAM

St Paul's Church

Railway

Tunnel

Golf Course

Flint House

comes out to a wider lane where we turn left to St Paul's Church, Woldingham.

Built in 1933, this church is well worth a visit. The bluish agates set in the inscription above the altar were a gift from Hyderabad, and the stained glass windows above the altar depict the sea in various moods. The roof timbers of Columbian pine support concealed lighting and the windows are surrounded with dressed flints.

Leaving the church on our left we continue along the road to Woldingham Green and turn left down Upper Court Road. Just past a house called Sylvan Mount we turn left down a steep path, passing a house on the right at the bottom of the dip. We cross the lane to Southview Road and just past a house turn slightly left to a signposted footpath.

We follow this path for about half a mile, at first along the edge of trees and finally uphill with trees eventually on our left, and over stiles out to a road. We cross over and turn left to admire the view over Oxted from the old road, following it to a road junction where we take the road signposted Oxted and Limpsfield. We continue on this road for a short distance then take a footpath on the left downhill to the top of the downs for views and a rest.

Retracing our steps back to the road we turn right and back to the crossroads and cross over to Flint House Lane, the bridleway to Warlingham, passing Flint House on the left. We continue straight ahead along this bridleway for a good mile. The last half mile of the path has woods on our right and is often rather muddy, but we eventually emerge at the top of a wide sloping field and go downhill on a clear path and out to the road.

Here we turn right passing some houses and later opposite Warren Barn Farm we turn left along Upland Road. At the T junction we turn right along a pleasant residential road out to Slines Oak Road. Here we cross to a bridleway opposite which takes us uphill and finally back to the green space opposite the bus garage.

Refreshments: Confectionery and ice cream at Woldingham village and Chelsham.

*

91

COUNTRY CODE

1. Guard against all risks of fire.
2. Fasten all gates.
3. Keep dogs under proper control.
4. Keep to the paths across farmland.
5. Avoid damaging fences.
6. Leave no litter.
7. Safeguard water supplies.
8. Protect wild life, wild plants and trees.
9. Go carefully on country roads.
10. Respect the life of the countryside.